FACING THE PUBLIC

Martina Evans

Facing the Public

ANVIL PRESS POETRY

Published in 2009
by Anvil Press Poetry Ltd
Neptune House   70 Royal Hill   London   SE10 8RF
www.anvilpresspoetry.com

Copyright © Martina Evans 2009

This book is published with financial assistance
from Arts Council England

Designed and set in Monotype Bembo by Anvil

ISBN 0 85646 412 6

A catalogue record for this book
is available from the British Library

to Tom and Marie Cotter

ACKNOWLEDGEMENTS

Some of these poems have previously appeared in these magazines: *Ambit*, *The Bow-Wow Shop*, *City Lighthouse* poetry anthology, *Magma*, *Oxford Magazine*, *The Rialto*, *Southward*.

'Grey Mare' was published in *All Alcoholics Are Charmers* (1998) and 'Jaunty' in *The Iniscarra Bar and Cycle Rest* (Rockingham Press, 1995).

The author gratefully acknowledges bursaries from the Irish Arts Council/An Chomhairle Eilaíon and Arts Council England and would also like to thank the Royal Literary Fund for its assistance.

Contents

Two Hostages 9

The Boy from Durras 11

Reprisal 12

Omar Khadr 13

Court Welfare Officer 14

Grey Mare 16

A Man's World 18

Western Heroes 19

Royalty 20

Cowboys 22

Jaunty 23

Desperate Men 24

Convert 25

Rounds 26

Every Year She Said 27

Facing the Public 28

The Height of the Crows 30

Stones 31

Ivy on the Wall 32

The Australian Rug 33

Style 34

Tonsillectomy 35

The Blue Room 36

Boa Constrictor 37

When I Opened My Prayer Book 38

My Last Confession 39

The King is Dead 40

Worried 1970 42

The Kill 43

Vegan   44

Bloody Mary   46

Goodnight Irene   47

Brakes   48

Falling   49

Hair   50

Gentrification   51

Wheels   52

Lefties   53

The 50th Anniversary of the Easter Rising   54

Mallow Burns, 28th September 1920   56

Wooden Horse   58

Subject Race   59

Knock   60

Two Hostages

In the photo
six bouncing babies, bonneted, sitting
in a pram outside Hackney Workhouse: 1902.
This was the year my father was born.
I have held his powder-blue
vaccination certificate issued
in that year by what was later
considered an alien government.
Could any of these babies come out of Hackney
to put on the Black and Tan uniform?
Bomb us now
was the sign on the Crossley Tender,
their bayonets pointed at my father
his hands tied over his head
his thin eighteen-year old body swaying
against the wire netting of the truck
as it drove past my grandmother
who must have remembered,
as she looked up startled,
all those days she carried him
bonneted, protected in her arms.

In 1921 my two-year-old mother
toddling outside my other grandmother's shop
was picked up by another Crossley Tender.
And this grandmother pursuing the truck
down the long village street

NOTE The Black and Tans were a mercenary military police force sent
by Lloyd George in 1920 to put down the Irish rebellion. They drove
special trucks known as Crossley Tenders.

9

knew that these hated men from the trenches
had shot children
and old men working in the fields
dragged a priest by a rope for sixty miles
wrecked homes never once forgetting
to crush the pictures of Virgin
and Sacred Heart under their heel.
They came like pirates with patches over their eyes
hooks instead of hands, tormented minds
tormenting the people they hunted like game
as they drank, swore, swaggered, cocked their pistols
and made the people kneel to sing
God Save the King.
How could she even breathe now as she stopped
outside Sheehy's pub, going inside
to discover my mother sitting on the counter
like a queen, drinking red lemonade
surrounded by those same dark faces
queuing up like suitors,
one of them claiming that he couldn't *get over*
the brown eyes of the Irish
and as my grandmother reported afterwards,
every single word out of his mouth
spoken in the language of Cockney.

The Boy from Durras

Yes, that's right, the Tans picked up children
and you know why of course, don't you?
They were looking for information.
I'll tell you something now on the quiet
and you'll get no one round here
to talk about it. No, they wouldn't open their mouths.
There was a young fellow picked up outside Durras.
He was sent down from the house.
I'd say only about twelve or thirteen,
not much more, sent down to the shop to get the messages.
And the Tans picked him up, gave him a lift to the shop.
Whether he said something or not was never known.
There's no point in asking me
and you won't get anyone round here to talk about it.
There was an IRA safe house raided that night, anyway
a truck load of the Boys taken to Bandon Barracks.
Well, you wouldn't want to be arrested by the Essex
          Regiment
no sir, fingernails pulled off and a slow death by the barracks
          fire —
they were very fond of the red hot poker, the Essex were.
Did the boy give them a tip-off? No one knows.
You'll get no one round here to talk about it today.
And it's seventy years on.
No, a crowd from the village came for the boy.
The parents couldn't save him, he was tied to a horse
and cart and dragged, yes the very same that the Tans
done to that priest outside Dunmanway, he was dragged
as far as Dromore before they stopped.
I'd say that's a distance of about forty mile.
And don't forget that you never heard this from me.

Reprisal

Never trust a Palatine or a Bastard –
and Ould Fritz was both.
When the Boys went to Ould Fritz
demanding their guns in the name of the Irish Republic –
I'll give you ammunition says Ould Fritz,
sticking his gun out of the window.
He shot Joe Bennett stone dead.
Bang. No more than he was a dog.
They wrapped his body in a sheet
put it in a ditch two miles from his home place
because the Tans were down to the house straight.
The Bennetts killed a pig, letting on nothing –
if the Tans found a corpse
they'd be burnt to the ground.
Mrs Bennett, standing there, stuffing sausages
her seventeen-year-old son's body lying in a ditch.
No more than he was a dog.
Those fellas going round the house
sticking their bayonets into everything.
Ould Fritz? Well he didn't leave his house
for fear of the Boys, two whole years getting
everything delivered and everyone laughing
at the big head of him inside the windows.
Of course they got him,
didn't he have to leave the house for his sister's funeral?
All the gentry assembled below in Askeaton Graveyard.
Bang. No more than he was a dog.
Four black horses with feathers going one way
and the hearse going the other.

Omar Khadr

There is video evidence of Omar at twelve,
wiring explosives laid out like cakes
on a tablecloth, his brown face
young and clear under his white kufi,
little boy fingers winding the wire,
white teeth biting the thread
before he was captured
at 15, in the broken-biscuit dust
of a blasted Afghan compound
exit wounds on his chest spreading
and red as blooming poppies.
They won't treat his wounds
until he talks someone has to sing
for the twin towers and Canada won't
extradite him, his family a national
embarrassment, Jihadic mother and
sister speaking out of raven black cloth,
ticking off what every boy should learn –
swimming, sniping, and horseback riding.
In Guantánamo, it's stress positions, orange jump
suits, interrogators calmly recording him
crying out for his mother.
When he's finally asked what he wants
he says car magazines, colouring books
and pencils, any kind of juice
as long as it is really weird.

Court Welfare Officer

Your teacher said we could talk in the café,
it is a marvellous building isn't it?
Aren't you lucky to be going to a school like this?
Purdy's for you and a tea for me.
You like Purdy's, do you?
Isn't that ceiling marvellous?
You know the restoration work here is an inspiration.
Mmm. Well!
So why don't you want to see your father?
You just don't want to, is that what you are saying.
Just you don't want to.
Well, you were all talk when I met you at home on Tuesday.
How come you can't say anything now?
You are afraid of him?
You'll have to tell me more than that.
I have to tell the judge more than that, you know.
I can't understand why you've suddenly gone so quiet.
You were all talk yesterday about your drama class.
The judge will bend over backwards to get you to see him.
You know that, don't you?
You will have to go into a room with him.
What's not safe about it?
It's nothing to worry about, I'll be there too.
You have got to say more than you are saying if you want me
        to take you seriously.
Do you know it is your dad who pays the school fees?
He told me himself, yesterday.
He is very sad and I feel very sorry for him.
Yes, I think it's very sad that you won't see him when he is
        paying the fees.

Look at that beautiful ceiling and the stained glass windows.
Drink up, now. I have to go soon.
I can't go back to the judge and tell him nothing, you know.
It's not fair, the judge will say I am not doing my job
    properly.
You need to finish up that drink.
You must have something more to say.
I will be told that I am not doing my job properly.
And you will have to leave your drink behind you.

Grey Mare

i. m. Thomas Cotter 1900–1979

After the Truce
his prison letter
was all about
his dream about
her.

Coming first
in the mare and brood class
at Newcastle,
his bursting pride
leading her into the ring
with colours up.

Afterwards,
awake in the cell,
his fear for her leg
was stronger
than his hope
for 'a grand and glorious peace.'

She was the first person he called on
the night of his escape.

In the seventies
he was an old fighter,
the same age as the century
hook nose
burnt brown eyes

whiskey head
tobacco fingers.

Yellow riding boots
with elasticated sides,
morning or evening,
wedding or funeral
always on his feet.

He was ready for her
the day she'd come again
drumming her hooves.

A Man's World

He could not bear it – a convent funeral,
his female relatives had to chivvy him along.
His cousin Sister Lazarian laid out
in a sky-blue Child of Mary cloak
with a face like a hawk sticking out
of the coffin. The slippery polished floors,
the green crochet-covered bell rope
hanging like a rebuke in the gloom.
He did not go to Mass.
The tapestries, embroidered swans on cushions
pictures of bishops and saints, tea and sandwiches.
There would be *No smoking*.
And yet, the pale eager faces of the nuns –
down the clean corridors the black habits swirled
and skirled. He knew it was party
when the fine white fingers poured Scotch
into a heavy glass right up to the top.
Asking questions about the races,
Tipperary's chances in the All Ireland.
In this purified atmosphere
he was an interesting man
with an interesting smell.
He lit a Sweet Afton and flicked ash
into the hand-held ashtray beside him,
sat back as the coifed and veiled women
arranged themselves around the room
preparing to be mesmerised.

Western Heroes

They sit under John Wayne,
Henry Fonda, Warren Oates,
thin obedient ears, large eyes
pooled under soft fringes,
they whinny and trot and gallop
and canter and rear
when it's called for
swim the Rio Grande, roll under
Apaches, fall with the stunt riders
off the bridge in *The Wild Bunch*,
endure pistol shots, sizzling explosives,
Mexicans, the prancing of Steve McQueen
in *The Magnificent Seven*,
the Civil War in *Shenandoah*,
the beauty, the terror and foam,
smell of horse sweat
and salty popcorn washed down with Coke.
These fellows know the sound
of a Winchester 73
or a Colt 45 as well as they know
the sound of their own hoof beats
and they keep galloping
clouds of dust now across Monument Valley.
They never lose their balance.

Royalty

*It was Jim McMahon who first pointed out
that you never come across a bald tinker,
nor do you ever see one in old age.*

— BERNARD O'DONOGHUE

For pure glamour, in my mind
no one could or will
beat the tinkers.
They were outsiders for a start,
sartorial smart, with an edge,
like the dangerous whiff
of burnt rubber you get at the Bumpers.
The young men, sometimes small,
always slim in leather jackets,
torn denim before it became *de rigueur*,
had unforgettable names
like Elvis O'Donoghue
Christy O'Driscoll the Bowler.
Even when I was ten
every one of them called me *ma'am*.
The older men, Teds or Rockers,
sported the sidelocks of Victorian cads,
with rubbery Native American skin
hair dyed blonde, they drove low
windowless vans and knew everything
about antiques and horses.
They were champion bowlers,
they spoke their own ancient language.
Even the people who abhorred them
barred them from pubs and shops,

would stop sometimes to whisper
in tones of mystified respect:

See that fellow over there
with the big head of white hair
he's the King of the Tinkers.

Cowboys

They came with a horse box
a present for Daddy they said, as he followed
them into the bar. Captain Lyley's face plummy
with drink, Uncle Tommy in shades of brown
and beige, his nicotine fingers, tan ankle boots,
Fry's Chocolate Cream tie.
I circled the yard in excitement, would I be throwing
my leg over a horse, soon? Billy the Kid lepping on
after bursting out of Lincoln Jail.
Taut and grave, I was more like Pat Garrett when
I stole near the box in my sandals,
my hat hanging down my back on its string.
Shouldn't a horse whinny or paw the ground with spirit?
Shouldn't I be able to see the points of her ears
as she tossed her head above the opening?
I pressed my own ear against the petrol-smelling wood.
Soft breathing and slight shifting,
maybe she was a Shetland.
Overhead the crows circled like buzzards.
The yard was deserted, it could have been *High Noon*
but it was dark when they finally came out of the bar
and Uncle Tommy fumbled with the bolts.
A little Dexter cow he announced to myself and Daddy.
The small donkey-brown figure stood
timid and still in the dim light of the BP pump.
Off to one side, Captain Lyley had Mammy's hands
in both of his, saying *Mrs Cotter, I am loath to leave you.*
No one noticed Daddy and me. Our murderous looks.

Jaunty

Light strikes the clock!
I've waited five hours
for you to come
crashing in,
apologising,
kissing my feet,
and jaunty.

Jaunty! I'll give you
jaunty – I've waited
while my mouth dried up –
a wrinkled raisin of fear –

saw the crash
put you in the ambulance
attended the funeral
bawled at the grave
comforted the orphan
collected the insurance –

all these long
clock ticking hours
till you came in,
apologising,
kissing my feet,
and jaunty.

Desperate Men

Christmas Day and Good Friday
were the only days that the pub closed.
And yet they came –
trembling strangers, under hats and caps,
lapels turned up against the slanting wind
or hiding a dog collar.
They were desperate.
We knew men like them for 363 days of the year
apologetic, obsequious and persistent,
dark ravens
tap tap tapping at our front door.
Isn't it a fright? everyone whispered
over the Brussels sprouts, *the one day in the year.*
Wouldn't you think they would stock up or their wives could . . .?
I pondered but *sshhh in the name of God* my mother
looked at me as if I was planning my future.
You'll draw them in on top of us,
she passed out slices of turkey on tip-toe
and we avoided the noise of cutlery on china
chewing tensely until we heard the sound
of footsteps on gravel again
the wind-up growl of an old Escort or Cortina starting up,
driving away.

Convert

When Captain Lyley told the Canon
he was thinking of converting,
the ecclesiastical carpet was rolled
right out. Talks at the presbytery
over sherry, the horsey priest nodding
away, hardly able to believe his luck,
Captain confessing to a feeling –
something missing in his life –
impressed by the deep faith of his Catholic neighbours –
these neighbours whose heads craned now
to see him at Mass, spreading out his silk handkerchief
before going down on one knee, sniffing incense,
ceremoniously folding ebony rosary beads
back into his empty wallet.
The captain had three horses to sell
and six weeks was just long enough
for the Canon to buy the mare,
arrange a good price for the other two.
Six weeks for the captain to realise that
he didn't have it in him after all – time
for the Canon to find out who'd really
been biting at the end of the line.

Rounds

for Jane

The sound of running feet
and the bang of the cash register,
Mammy forcing a fiver into Daddy's wallet,
to sit there all night smiling at people
and not to put your hand in your pocket to buy a drink.
This was the second round of a battle.
The first round was getting him into a bath
then his fawn sports coat and olive-green knitted tie.
His rosy face shone after the forced shaving
and through the shop window I watched
his instinctively polite gentlemanly gestures
as Pat Shea solicitously settled him into the car.
God Almighty! said Mammy when he arrived back later
and she caught him placing his smooth intact fiver
under the spring in the drawer.
But still Pat Shea called for him delightedly
every Sunday night. After the sound of running feet,
Mammy flying at the cash register, springing
the drawer open, pursuing him with a crumpled fiver,
begging him *in the name of God* to stand his round.

Every Year She Said

If I have to cook Christmas dinner again
I will go off my head! But all she did was rattle
cutlery in the background, tell long winding stories.
It was my sisters' and sisters-in-law's woolly backs
that bent over the roast and the potato croquettes.
God I can't stand Christmas she said as she
avoided the decorating and even Daddy went
weird running away when we asked him
to cut down a Christmas Tree. He slapped the naked
turkey and laughed when Ber and I said
we couldn't bear the pimpled flesh.
Well I have to have a lie down anyway. She went
away with a Stations of the Cross face after dinner
leaving us miserable and stuffed as turkeys
down in the dark and shuttered bar.
I put the ball of my fist in my mouth when Rhett
told Scarlett he frankly didn't give a damn
and the light from the black and white telly
flickered sadly across our faces.
Come on throw on your things she'd be standing
there then with no respect for the television,
her tweed coat swinging open and the keys jangling
in her hand. *There's nothing like a good walk*
for the health of the mind. We walked the bare
North Cork roads under skeletal trees, noted
the rowan, the wren and the fox. *Thanks be to God*
I've put another Christmas dinner behind me –
she thanked God a lot on that fresh and foggy walk
until finally, our heads full of tingling cold fire,
we burst through the bar door
hungry for ham and mustard sandwiches.

Facing the Public

My mother never asked like a normal person, it was
I'm asking you for the last time, I'm imploring you
not to go up that road again late for Mass.

She never had slight trouble sleeping, it was
Never, never, never for one moment did I get a wink,
as long as my head lay upon that pillow.

She never grumbled, because *No one likes a grumbler,*
I never grumble but the pain I have in my two knees this night
there isn't a person alive who would stand for it.

She didn't just have an operation; she died in the Mercy Hospital
and came back to life only when Father Twohig beckoned
from the foot of her blood-drenched bed.

She didn't just own a shop and a pub, she told bemused
     waitresses
that she was *running a business in the country, urgently*
when she insisted that we were served first.

She didn't do the Stations of the Cross
she sorrowed the length and breadth of the church.
And yet, she could chalk up a picture in a handful of words

conjure a person in a mouthful of speech; she took off her
     customers
to a T, captivating us all in the kitchen,
drawing a bigger audience than she bargained for.

How often we became aware of that silent listener
when he betrayed himself with a creak, a sneeze or a cough.
How long had he been standing, waiting in the shop?

We looked at each other with haunted faces,
and I, being the youngest, got the job of serving him
his jar of Old Time Irish, his quarter pound of ham,

writing his messages into The Book, red-faced and dumb
before his replete and amused look.
Meanwhile, inside, my mother held a tea towel to her brow.

Never, never, never would she be able, as long as she lived,
even if she got Ireland free in the morning, no, no, no
she would never be able to face the public again.

The Height of the Crows

in memory of Elizabeth Cotter 1865–1935

I open the window, look down the drop
to where the bulbs are coming up –
yellow white and green splashes on the brown earth.
Beside me, Alice's moist nose points like a pistol.
A crow caws by and she snaps her head round
like a whip. Her whiskers tremble.
Caw, caw. The sound is lonely and homely.
I smell the early mornings going to Burnfort School,
see the line of trees beyond the priest's house,
remember the farm where my father grew up.
Ard na Preachán – the height of the crows.
Here stable doors hung splintered as hangnails,
the only horses were photos on the wall.
Whiskey steamed in my uncle's teacup.
Once, someone pointed to the outline of a garden
that Granny Cotter had worked. All that day
I walked around the remains of a miniature hedge.
On an Edwardian morning with weather like this,
she might have watched Sibey's neck snap
to attention as crows caped past, caw caw
villainous, homely, familiar
cries that last.

Stones

As a child, I craved straight lawns and brick walls,
house names like Sorrento or Saint Anthony of Padua.
I loved the neat Council flats of pink blue and yellow,
their lines of washing seemed to flag up sophistication
as we passed through the outskirts of Cork.
There was nothing pretty or holy about the names
of the two farms in our family — *Ard na Preachán* and *Cloch* —
The Height of the Crows and Stones.
Cloch, the haunted one, was sold
but its stories itched the family —
the horse that went mad from a brain haemorrhage
circling and circling around the hawthorn-ringed field,
the riding accidents, bodies on the railway tracks,
Johnny the dead dog the children buried up to his neck.
So used to the phantom footsteps on the stair
they must have thought the dead went on living.
Unable to smother his beloved head in earth, they thought
Johnny should be able to see and hear and smell,
or even bark which was what my mother thought
when she came around the corner,
saw him staring at her there, his head disembodied
a fly-eyed, stone-headed idol, flat on the ground.

Ivy on the Wall

Four storeys high, a foot,
even a foot and a half thick
in some places, green, glossy
and when the wind passed through
you could hear the sea. *Listen, listen to it,*
I kept saying. It was at a time
when nothing would grow for me
nothing except that wall of green.
When I was told that it wasn't neighbourly
I had to be brave but the man I hired
to cut the root turned away, cried,
said that he was sick in his stomach.
As if the vet had broken down
in the middle of putting down the cat,
as if I had asked the man to cut the heart
out of Snow White. I helped him carry
the thick trunk, branches like arms and legs
some as thick as thighs, we were like
murderers. The leaves are turning brown now,
it is dying, although at night-time
the dark leaves could pass for green.
Last night, I lay on the ground on my back
and the shifted view made it look like a field
or a fairytale steep thicket,
almost a miracle, except for the TV aerial
that forms a steel cross, a grave marker
at the very top.

The Australian Rug

Some visitors brought it
years ago. It was made of cashmere
I think, too good anyway
for picnics, my mother said.
Fawn and milky cocoa-coloured
pink-brown and cream, it smelled
sweet and nutty like those
soft toy-like kangaroos, koalas and wallabies
I imagined far below my Corkonian feet,
hopping along in a hot dream world of gum trees
where the kookaburra laughed his head off.
My father's lips pursed with pleasure
when he uttered the name of a place called Geelong,
as if he was getting ready to blow
into an invisible didgeridoo.
I put my nose to the rug's folded sweetness,
whispering
kangaroo, koala, wallaby,
thinking of the picnics to come
when the rug would be old enough
to take out and spread down by the river.
Years later, searching in the Hot Press,
I found it, still folded, old and strangely
odourless. The moths had eaten right through
and when I opened it up, the holes formed
a pattern like those snowflakes and stars
we made out of paper years ago.

Style

Weeks spent watching my hair beginning
to soften, curl against my yellow viyella
collar flicking it back, tossing it in front
of the walnut wardrobe in the big bedroom.
Sometimes I'd wear a towel around my head
streaming down my shoulders, patting
the heads of the mink stole lying across my lap.
The tan and the sharp black crocodile handbags
smelling of old powder, full of thin blue air-mail letters
and photos from Australia where they all lived before
I ever existed, with or without long hair.
Sometimes I creaked open the bottom drawer
pored over photographs of nuns with habits
and large architectural wimples.
My towel could be a veil, too.
I tightened it around my face.
Maybe I'd be a nun. I lifted a ruler
carved with Aboriginal designs from the dresser.
If I was that good, I wouldn't fear Hell
or the footsteps on the stairs
the firm triumphant shouts
as I was dragged out, sobbing
from behind the wardrobe.
I was on my way to the hairdresser whether
I liked it or not and besides it was a well known fact
that cutting it all off had a strengthening effect
on a head of hair.

Tonsillectomy

Nuala bought the slippers with puppy ears
and eyes that went from side to side.
She packed the blue weekend case
and Mammy walked me up the brick path
to Mount Alvernia.
She asked me twice if I was lonely
but I couldn't speak.
Do you know who I am?
The anaesthetist approached my trolley,
he was the terrifying stranger
I'd seen in the kitchen
his moustache dipped in a pint of Guinness
late on Hallowe'en night.
You're the mask, I slurred before
waking to acres, a farm of soreness
in my throat and four strange children in the room.
The oldest was a boy and he took charge.
Behind the locked door in the corner
he said there was a dying man
with eyes like strawberry jam
and the hand of a skeleton.
He got out of his bed to rattle
the handle of the door,
the rest of us too sore to tell him stop.
The nurse came in the end,
told us we were a disgrace.
That room, she said,
was as empty now
as the backs of our scraped-out throats.

The Blue Room

The fourth wall was dark
pine ship's panelling
rescued from a wreck
although I didn't know that then
and how in the end everything
ends up a wreck.
Or maybe I did know because
I was afraid of my own skeleton
buried not too deep under my flesh
only waiting for its chance
to peep out and grin horribly at me.
Sometimes a bit of light came through
the glass panel high up
and I could hear the creak of boards
and the patter of mice. Sometimes
the singing voices from the bar were very near,
they sang *A Nation Once Again* which was
companionable. Or *I'm nobody's child*
which was like a soundless hole in my throat
and sometimes
they didn't sing only mumbled and the voices
were very far away and snakes and devils crowded
the room. What was a snake's skeleton like?
The only cure then, as now,
was books, books, books –
kneeling at the window sill
the *Major* cigarettes sign
lighting up the page
with electric green and white light.

Boa Constrictor

It was the picture of Saint Patrick
driving out the snakes
that kept them on my mind.
If they were here before
what was to stop them coming back?
The one I had in mind didn't even
have to cross the sea. I could see clearly
the big fat body of him that I last saw rearing
against the thick glass in Dublin zoo.
I saw the road from Dublin disappearing
under his muscular body as he went past
signposts, no need for such a diabolical fellow
to check where he was going –
cleverly travelling at night, arranging himself
carefully in ditches for sleep by day.
Every so often, he might stop to open his mouth for
        a sheep like
the picture I'd seen in World Book Encyclopaedia.
He knew where he was coming all right –
the village of Burnfort.
I was there in the dark, the lights from the cars
travelling across the room in white bands,
a knitting needle like a sliver of ice
clenched in my right hand.

When I Opened My Prayer Book

I saw him on the page
his body flesh like bright burning coal
his arrow tail sizzling
right beside Mrs Mullane
in her 1940s costume suit,
her ripple-curled hair gripped with clips
beside Tom Twomey down on one knee
its arthritic roundness
cradled in his soft cloth cap.
Mesmerized women were hissing
along the length of their rosaries
under Father O'Shea's meditative drone
and comforting stutter.
Right in the middle of these solid people
heaving with belief
right between the white leatherette covers of my missal
he was confident,
smirking in the knowledge
that he'd always be with me
even though I would have a whole pile of trouble
believing in the existence of God.

My Last Confession

He wasn't what you'd want to look at –
orange hair sprayed in a thick beard
over his brown robes and in between the toes
of his Franciscan leather sandals –
but he told us boarders
that we were misunderstood angels
and that the nuns didn't understand him either.
Of course we should be allowed to drink altar wine
confess openly away from restraints
in the library.
I thought he was the liberated uncle I never had
so when he asked me to sit on his lap
I was genuinely sorry that I couldn't oblige.
I'm too heavy I confessed.
You're grand he said softly.
No matter how often he repeated it –
You're grand, you're grand, you're grand
in the name of God
aren't I telling you you're grand? –
and he was nearly shouting in the end.
I stayed on my knees.
Bless me father for I have sinned
it was eleven years before I remembered –
and it struck me
as I walked down Charing Cross Road,
that once, for ten minutes in 1977
God might have been watching over me.

The King is Dead

The deep Radio Luxembourg voice announced it
like it was an ad for a film. And then
it was *Blue Suède Shoes* and *Return to Sender*
and the voice again, saying it like that
The King is Dead.
I'm in the old dining room, peering down
at the bar where a few voices flow under one loud one.
Do they know? *The King is Dead.*
They don't know. I could be the one
to announce it. I could walk down into the bar now
and say it: *The King is Dead.* But they might say
I am stupid or that I am trying to be smart
which I am, of course.
The first one in Burnfort to break the news –
who do I think I am? *Love me Tender.*
I touch the worn velvet table cloth,
the tin cash box, the plastic fruit.
The King is Dead. I start my journey
but stop by the box of penny bars in the shop.
Retreat, unwrapping a raspberry split.
Look at my face in the brown sideboard mirror.
I've been told I've been wrong so often,
I don't believe my ears
peeping through my long hair.
And besides, that voice – *The King is Dead*
the voice of an advertiser if ever I heard one.
Thinning voices as the last people drift away
to the noisy hint of washing glasses,

the bolts running home. I mount the stairs
thinking of how I've missed my chance
and wake in the morning
to my mother's announcement
that the whole world is talking about it.

Worried 1970

for Ber

I don't know why, maybe she needed me as a witness but for some reason, Ber brought me downstairs to the bathroom in the early hours. We turned right two thirds of the way down the staircase, passed in front of the long mirror, where the staircase separated, three steps down to stand in our bare feet on the cold moist red tiles in front of the open frosted window. *Here Brownie, Brownie, Brownie, come on Brownie, Brownie Brownie.* I shivered in my yellow brinylon night-dress as he half-ambled, half-wriggled his way up to the window where it opened onto the yard; his belly close to the ground and his head even lower, the shamed look he had when his brown eyes met her brown eyes. She beat him then and there and her hand must have been burning and it seems to me her tears were burning, too, but I couldn't have known that, for surely it wasn't I that was crying? And surely, I was thinking, as she must have been thinking, that he would learn his lesson now: *Keep away from those other dogs.* They were the *wrong crowd, a bad influence.* Sooner or later he would get caught, put down or even shot on the run. Surely, now he would stop coming back, bloodstained and ashamed, looking hunted when it was he was the one who was worrying Susie's sheep?

The Kill

Screaming *Susie Susie* I ran up the ruined steps that led to
nowhere and stood there with my hands in my mouth. I
understood now what feathers flying meant. I was stand-
ing in a blizzard, Brownie's lupine jaws around their rust
and white squawking necks. Why pick this moment? After
all those evenings when he trotted by my side under the
green beech tunnels, me in my red coat with my basket of
eggs and canister of milk. Looking up brown-eyed and
kind at Susie as she patted his rough coat. The yard was
black with cars when I took a running leap from the
crumbling steps throwing myself against the familiar high-
latched door. Howling *Susie Susie Susie* bruising my hands
against the wood. Darkness picking out the shadows one
by one as everything became grey and quiet. Did he know
that they couldn't stop in the middle or was Brownie able
to gauge the exact decibel of prayer needed to drown out
the sound of the kill?

Vegan

for Siobhan

I want my trace
on the earth to be as light
as a strand of gossamer. Superfoods.
Nuts and berries, mushrooms
on toast. Chestnuts,
chick pea curries. Who wouldn't be satisfied
with that or want to steal the milk
out of a calf's pink mouth?

Red wine, too.
Simple fruits made into
a satisfying drink, red and hearty
without any slaughter. Drink up
it's good for your heart and
animal-loving soul and full no doubt
of other good things you've yet
to read about in the papers.

When you've had a good few
and your friends are saying that
they haven't the will power
you'll find that you're not meeting
their eyes, your nose is more of a snout
now because you're the first
person to notice the cocktail sausages
circling on silver trays

like ballroom dancers around the room
you can't stop
your tail wagging at the waiters
you can't even think
you're quickly apologising
for what you are about to eat
then digging in
like a right animal.

Bloody Mary

Justin's favourites
were small, dark-haired
they wore creamy trench coats
neat suits, they never had to ask
for a Bloody Mary.

Within minutes of their arrival
it would be glowing in a tall glass
on the shining formica bar counter:
Britvic tomato, Worcester sauce, vodka,
black pepper and celery salt
stirred with a clanking tall spoon.

His hard brown eyes, his distant voice
What do you want?
were the first sign of a fall from favour.
Most knew better than to ask
while others clung in disbelief
to the remnants of their glorious past.

'Don't you know it's a Bloody Mary,
Justin?' 'A Bloody Mary?'
would be the loud astonished reply
as if Justin had been woken in the middle of night
and asked to dig a grave.
The ex-favourite would have to sit
through the reluctant clattering of spoon and glass
everyone looking on
watching her force herself to drink her last one
when she couldn't even stomach it.

Goodnight Irene

i.m. Irene Cotter 1921–2007

Two words and I'm back
Burnfort Bar 1976 – the men have broken
into the raggle-taggle chorus
quit your rambling, quit your gambling
quit staying out late at night.
Mammy laughs *I won't be soft-soaped*
into doing after hours.

Further back, I'm small enough
to stand under the cold marble fireplace.
Mammy's not laughing, she's telling
about 1950. Every time it came on
her mother turned off the wireless.
Mammy was in Australia,
they never saw each other alive again.

If Irene turns her back on me, I'm gonna
jump in the river and drown. 2007.
Martin Harley singing in the Royal Oak.
I stumble down the stairs onto Hill Street,
stand smoking under a full moon.
The song follows, a dog barks
and I can't turn anything off.

Brakes

Mammy said that I'd have to cut it out right now.
Cycling together. I was singing under the tunnel of beeches
and gasping on the hill as I dragged the tarmac

with my foot. I was ten, there were no brakes on my bike.
Paddy Casey took off his cap, wiped his sweat
and took it all in. He was in the shop by evening.

Mrs Cotter, they're no better than tramps. T'anam an Diabhal.
My soul to the devil. I'd have to cut it out right now.
But we'd sat down by the hay bales, he'd opened

a bottle of Time beer and put his hand on my ankle.
At the pump house the freshly ironed butterfly motifs
came away from the knees of my brown bell bottoms.

I sat on the stone wall saying no more, I couldn't
see him no more, couldn't look at him or explain about Mammy
and Paddy talking about his soul and the devil.

Falling

for Catherine Maxwell

I am nine, half crying
outside Deanes' back door
the rainy dark November shiny
cobbles brown in the yard light
Mammy's down again
cracked her elbow this time.
Always falling, getting to her feet
cantering to her next accident.
Not long married when Daddy
asked her if she wasn't *a bit false in the legs.* –
As if he'd been landed with a bad filly!
she laughed. But she frightened
herself too as I frighten myself now.
November, month of the Holy Souls,
down I go time after time.
No time to grieve or remember
her only when my knee slaps
on the stone hearth, I stagger back
into the lemon balm, or my worn heels
bring me to my knees
on Kingsway.
A man with a gold ring
on every finger helps me to peel
my scattered papers from the wet pavement.
Resisting the urge to bless myself
I thank him, walk away.

Hair

for Liadáin

Never mattered as much
after those days at school
when once a week was all
we were allowed to wash it.
Girls tried out the new-fangled
aerosol can of *dry shampoo*,
looked prematurely aged
from the overuse of talc,
or hid greasiness in tight firm plaits.
Saturday morning, the whole dormitory
awoke and rustled with flowing water,
the opening and closing of taps.
Eyes pink from Sunsilk and Lorene
pairs of girls made their way
to the sun-filled windows of the top corridor
where they combed and teased the long
wet strands until they were dry as kindling, lighting up
with sunlight, spraying with electricity as if the hair
itself was reaching out to the life ahead.

Gentrification

for Mary Condé

Soon we won't be able to remember George
his yard like a tip strewed with parts of old cars
and radios, his many tenants, the favourite
who liked to take his yellow Escort greasily apart
on the pavement. George waving in the window
in striped pajamas, holding his toothbrush.
The homemade plumbing on public display,
the pipes that stuck right out of George's outside wall,
the appalling dead crow on a stick that made Líadáin
afraid to go out in the garden.
All gone, even the other tenant, the one
with the baritone who rose in the dark
mornings and sang, his voice going up and down
as he went from storey to storey.
The front door banging behind him,
he went, still singing down the road,
his voice disappearing into the mist
as he signalled with open and expansive hands.

Wheels

Eileen Murphy after a yellow homesick glance
went under the bed, turned her head away.
These two grey ones make no signs as we leave.
They are invisible long before the front door clicks
and why should they bid us goodbye anyway?
We return ill from plane, train, tube and bus
the thirsty dry haul through packed stations
where the whole world is pulling along
belongings in zipped boxes, all rattling
on ubiquitous cranky wheels.
They don't like the wheels either, crouch greyly
among the shadows until the noise stops and
they come shyly out of dark corners, arch
and sniff, listening intently as if our voices
are suddenly birdsong. Alice on the window sill
watching between the hot August geraniums
short soft paws tucked over the frame.
She presses down hard on the wood,
we smell different, changed.
She finds our presence a relief
and yet we all feel strange.

Lefties

What's Communism?
my daughter is
as confused in the nineties
as I was in the sixties.
It was like the Sixth Commandment
no one explained it –
a mysterious sinful disease
that was hinted at in Mass
and by nuns with tightened lips,
the first thing that the Virgin Mary broached
when she appeared in Fatima.
Pray for the defeat of Communism
she implored Lucia, Jacinta and Francisco
as the iron curtain swung strangely,
like a bell with no clapper
somewhere out there
beyond the West.
The first lefty I met
was an attractive brown-eyed man,
living in a tall house
with bookcases in the kitchen.
He had to flee Cork in the 50's
he was so left wing.
What's left wing, Mum?
I thought it must be
something desperate.
He'd buried two wives
and when his daughter asked
his new fiancée if she wasn't afraid
to marry him, the book-filled kitchen
exploded with laughter as if everyone knew
something I didn't.

50th Anniversary of the Easter Rising

Suddenly I was awake.
I put on my petticoat with the three frills,
Yellow, pink and blue.
I tied the big pin on my mustard pleated kilt.
As I combed my hair in the grey mirror, I noticed the silence.
Down the stairs in my white bobby socks
treading softly on the green battleship lino.
It took me a while to figure out that they'd left without me.
I stood in the empty bar and the lager was dull gold in the dim
    light.
I couldn't believe it at first.
Didn't they know how much I was looking forward?
The Thomas Davis piper band out from Mallow
the waving of the green white and gold
the old IRA closing one eye to fire shots over the monument.
Years later, I saw shaky old men who could hardly lift their
    rifles.

Years later I saw shaky old men who could hardly hold their
    rifles.
The old IRA closing one eye to fire shots over the monument
the waving of the green white and gold
the Thomas Davis piper band out from Mallow.
Didn't they know how much I was looking forward?
I couldn't believe it at first.
I stood in the empty bar and the lager was dull gold in the dim
    light.
It took me a while to figure out that they had left without me.
Treading softly on the green battleship lino,
I came down the stairs in my white bobby socks.

I noticed the silence as I combed my hair in the grey mirror.
I tied the big pin on my mustard pleated kilt.
I put on my petticoat with the three frills,
yellow pink and blue.
Suddenly I was awake.

Mallow Burns, 28th September 1920

'The people of Mallow, long a garrison town, were not friendly'

'The sheltering belly of our horse had paid for harbouring us'

           − ERNIE O'MALLEY, IRA Commander

9.30 am and the sun passes over the steeple of St Mary's
Church, swans on the Blackwater, smoking men leaning
against the Clock House, women in brown hats buying
milk in the creamery, skull and crossbones badges flashing
on the uniforms of the Lancers exercising their horses
along the Navigation Road as a solid gold bar of dust
breaks over Sergant Gibbs's khaki back and he bends over
the horse's hoof held up as dainty as a dancer beside the
fierce smithy blaze and the barracks quiet before the rapid
fire of footsteps on the stone corridors when he turns
from the horse hears the order *the Guard Room now, boys*
sees the trench-coated men leading his comrades but he
can't *Halt*, can't do it though they say they'll fire and the
first bullet goes through the sunbeam and the horse
shrieks and they shout *Halt* again and he shouts *No* elon-
gated and deep from his belly which becomes wet and
sticky as his head thuds against the jamb of the door and
he smells something more than horse sweat and someone
tries to bandage him and then their voices are getting faint
like horseflies buzzing away and they have 2 Hotchkiss
light machine guns 27 rifles 1 revolver very light pistols
4,000 rounds of ammunition a quantity of bayonets and
lances packed in three motors in under twenty minutes
and he won't hear one of them playing a melodeon on the
back of the car as they pass out of the town into the safe
countryside or the quiet all afternoon, late sun falling on
the black cloth of the Protestant minister and the Parish
Priest begging the Colonel in Buttevant for no reprisals

and the aeroplane that comes from Fermoy later again and circles over Mallow Barracks and drops a message and flies to Buttevant before going back to Fermoy and must be taking back the promise now because the sun is sinking into the Blackwater and the Lancers are stone drunk and they toss their cigarettes into the tide – a shower of loose red eyes – and the people are nailing galvanized zinc in front of their plate glass windows and soldiers are driving in from Fermoy and Buttevant and the sun goes finally down on two hundred years of loyalty to the Crown, all night under the moon, the white swans on the black water against the red sky, screams of the women, the creamery on fire, three hundred jobs gone, Town Hall flaming, houses alight, holy pictures bayoneted, the screams of the women, one pregnant lying down beside the grey stones in the graveyard and she'll be too cold the next time the sun rises to ever get up again.

Wooden Horse

'We're like the Greeks in the wooden horse, here in the belly
of the town, I thought, and laughed.'

           — ERNIE O'MALLEY

If you meet anyone, blindfold them, they were told that
and the men were smiling at the thought of seizing the
barracks where an officer was starting to write a letter
Mallow is a quiet town, nothing ever happens here. And it was
true — at 2 a.m. on the twenty eighth, there was no one
on the streets, everything pitch as they navigated back-
yards and barbed wire, put up their ladders against the
high walls. Up there, Ernie saw a toy town wrapped in
mist and when they clambered inside the Town Hall, he
laughed, thinking of Troy. He whispered the story to Dave
Shinnock who whispered it to the rest of men and they
never heard such a good joke and a boy slapped the thick
wall and said *now girl, whoa girl, steady there and made a wind*
purr with his mouth as if he was rubbing down a horse but
Mallow wasn't made of wood, it was flesh and blood, like
Achilles' horses, Bailius and Xanthus, who dragged their
shining manes along the ground when they wept for the
death of Patroclus.

Subject Race

We spare none of what quality or sex soever and it hath bred much terror in the people.

— SIR ARTHUR CHICESTER,
Lord Deputy of Ireland 1605–1616

This is Spenser's description of the Irish
he enthusiastically cleared
during the Plantation of Munster:
Out of every corner of the woods
and glens they came creeping forth
upon their hands, for their legs could
not bear them; they looked like anatomies
of death; they spake like ghosts crying
out of their graves. Chicester's soldiers
in the North laughed as they lured
toddlers to death by the sword
with meat roasted by camp fires. Helmet
heads laughing into their ruffs, the smell
of meat, babies butchered by the side
of the road, these Renaissance get-rich-quick
soldiers justified themselves —
weren't they civilising savages? But this is
what happens when a race is conquered:
rape, plunder, butchery and starvation so bad
people wait by the gallows to cut down corpses
and eat them in the dark.

Knock

Coughlin . . . helped to keep all in good humour, and his
droll sayings were repeated. He had been billeted in a house
which had a reputation for being stingy. One morning the
woman of the house asked him how he liked his eggs boiled.
"With a couple of others, ma'am," he replied.

        — ERNIE O'MALLEY, IRA Commander

No one wanted Ireland free more than myself, don't I
remember as a child, my mother grabbing hold of us,
making us lie down on the floor so we wouldn't be seen
by the landlord out for his day with the ducks in the bog
and his gun broken across his arm, looking to quench his
thirst with a glass of milk. *I say! Very refreshing indeed* and a
big slick of cream stuck to his old moustache. Ah those
days are gone, thanks be to God, old Pym would be afraid
of his life to come up to Knock in his plus fours now.
That's what I was thinking this morning and how great it
was to be able to open the bottom half of the door and
stand out on the flags in my sack apron, the tongues of my
boots hanging open with no laces. A brown cake baking
in the bastable pot and I tasting the air, like it was lemon-
ade. The sun was going across my shoulders like a warm
wool coat as I walked over to the henhouse with Blackie
the cat pressing up against me. And I was walking out
again with six hot white eggs in my big sack pockets,
thinking of the breakfast I was going to have with
Diarmuid. Well, whatever turn I made to admire the
heather blazing against the blue mountain, didn't I see a
crowd of them coming round the corner with the old
rifles upon their shoulders, singing *Oro Se De Bheath*

NOTE Knock: a common Irish place name. It comes from Cnoc
which means mountain.

Abhaile and my stomach sank to the tongues of my boots. Coughlin, the first as usual, to smell the brown cake. It wasn't that I wasn't wishing them the best of luck the whole time and you might think I'd be worried if we were caught out by the Tans and burned to the ground and I am not saying I wasn't always worried about that too, but to have turn around and serve a crowd of men and make up beds and to have to pretend to be laughing away at their jokes. Oh God Almighty, I was pure sick of them all then. I remember the first time they came and I was given a pile of dirty socks and Diarmuid handing the pile to me, like it was a chalice and I, like a mope, thinking it was some kind of an honour to be scraping the mud off them and when they were dry the next day, didn't I darn the lot of them like an even bigger mope. But this morning, anyway, I hid a couple of the eggs for ourselves and got a big pot of porridge going. 'Twas when Coughlin made his smart remark that I had to walk over to the fire because I thought I was going to cry and the only thing that cured me, as I was looking down into the bubbling oatmeal, was when I remembered being told how the waiters above in the Savoy Hotel in Cork might spit into the soup of customer if they took a turn against him. And I am still smiling now through my stupid old tears, sitting by the well in the dark, thinking of what I've just put between our sheets after my old mope, Diarmuid gave our bed away to Coughlin for the night. Diarmuid, of course, insisting, right go wrong, that it was a great honour and that it would make my day.

Also by Martina Evans from Anvil

᭺

All Alcoholics Are Charmers

Evans's great skill is in knowing how much to put into a poem. She has a talent for selecting only the most resonant memories, for not over-icing the cake of sentiment. . . . *All Alcoholics Are Charmers* turns out to be rich in splendidly concise evocations of what it feels like to be Irish in England, in all its quiddity, including the encounters with new cultures on your doorstep . . . Above all, Evans puts the right words in the right order, a dictum whose simple phrasing embodies its demands.

MICHAEL DUGGAN in *PN Review*

Can Dentists Be Trusted?

The poems take up the themes [of Evans's Irish child-hood and education in the 1960s] in funny yet disturbingly precise accounts of her parents, their sweet shop, recalcitrant cats, school ('filling the inkwells / from the greatest earthenware pot') and the monologues of Catholic mothers: '. . . and now Father Tim is all over the tabloids'. These look like easy, anecdotal poems but they bite.

ALAN BROWNJOHN in *The Sunday Times*